D1560931

# QUEEN
## A RHAPSODY

Publisher and Creative Director: Nick Wells

Project Editors: Laura Bulbeck and Polly Prior

Picture Research: Esme Chapman and Laura Bulbeck

Art Director: Mike Spender

Layout Design: Jane Ashley

Digital Design and Production: Chris Herbert

Special thanks to: Daniela Nava, Matt Knight, Victoria Menson, Frances Bodiam, Helen Crust

**FLAME TREE PUBLISHING**

Crabtree Hall, Crabtree Lane

Fulham, London SW6 6TY

United Kingdom

www.flametreepublishing.com

www.flametreerock.com

First published 2015

15 17 19 18 16

1 3 5 7 9 10 8 6 4 2

© 2015 Flame Tree Publishing Ltd

All rights reserved. No part of this publication may be reproduced, stored in a retrieval system, or transmitted in any form or by any means, electronic, mechanical, photocopying, recording or otherwise, without the prior permission in writing of the publisher.

A CIP record for this book is available from the British Library upon request.

ISBN 978-1-78361-306-9

Printed in China

# QUEEN
## A RHAPSODY

HUGH FIELDER

Foreword: Mark Beaumont

**FLAME TREE**
**PUBLISHING**

# CONTENTS

# FOREWORD

**M**ajestic, stately, a bona fide national treasure: no band was ever better named than Queen, or better read the currents of their time. They recognized the elemental power of Led Zeppelin's burgeoning hard rock scene, the grand pop scale of David Bowie's glam movement and the enormous ambitions of Pink Floyd's prog explosion, and plucked and wove these threads into a sumptuous robe that would enfold the globe, make every one of us feel like royalty.

Their modus operandi was all laid out in their signature tune – 1975's 'Bohemian Rhapsody', the six-minute thunderbolt that cemented their legend and fandango'd up every chart on the planet. It had the sprawling structure of an indulgent prog epic, but each 'movement' was a concise melodic pop piece at heart, forming the culmination of 1970s rock music and pointing the way to the grandiose chant rock to come. 'We Will Rock You', 'We Are The Champions', 'Bicycle Race', 'Radio Ga Ga', 'Flash', 'Don't Stop Me Now', 'One Vision', 'I Want It All' – songs designed to unite stadiums and celebrate the uncrushable spirit, music that floated on high above punk, new wave, the new romantics and the prog morass in its own gleaming bubble of pomp and glory.

And, at its centre, arguably the greatest rock'n'roll showman of the twentieth century. A human mirrorball, a strutting ringmaster, a tungsten glare of mustachioed charisma. Whether parading stages in twenty feet of ermine and velvet, bellowing his operatic octaves over some of the catchiest choruses of the 1970s, 1980s and 1990s or working tirelessly to his final moments to leave the greatest legacy possible, Freddie Mercury was a high-camp figurehead remembered far more for his talent, presence and supernova star quality than for the circumstances of his tragic early demise. In the Valhallan hallways of rock iconography, he proudly strides to this day, owning the place. Mercurial indeed.

Mark Beaumont

Journalist and Author

# HAPPY AND GLORIOUS

'YEARS AGO, I THOUGHT UP THE NAME QUEEN ... IT'S JUST A NAME, BUT IT'S VERY REGAL OBVIOUSLY, AND IT SOUNDS SPLENDID...'
FREDDIE MERCURY

When Queen burst on to the scene in the mid-Seventies, they changed the face of rock and roll – quite literally. Before Queen showed up, the rock scene had grown a serious face. There were heavy metal bands strutting defiantly to leaden riffs, blues rock bands with their interminable solos, supergroups locked in egocentric combat – often with themselves – progressive rock bands lost in the labyrinth of their concept albums, singer-songwriters gazing reflectively at their navels and one-dimensional pop groups frantically seeking their 15 minutes of fame. Even glam rock had become glum once pioneering stars like Marc Bolan and David Bowie had moved on, leaving the rest with increasingly fixed grins.

## Chemistry

Queen put the smile back on the face of rock and roll. They reminded everyone that it was, first and foremost, meant to be fun. And they succeeded beyond their wildest dreams. The proof of that is the power of the legacy that they have left behind, both tangible and intangible.

The key to the success of any band is invariably down to the chemistry between its members – something that is impossible to predict. There was nothing to suggest that the chemistry between Freddie Mercury, Brian May, Roger Taylor and John Deacon would produce what it did. However, Mercury's flamboyance, May's technical genius, Taylor's instinctive feel for rock and roll, and Deacon's introverted rock and roll sense gelled with remarkable results.

Although Mercury soaked up the limelight as the group's frontman, within the band the four-way dynamic reigned supreme. And it never faltered. With most bands, the dynamic changes with success, which can often be a source of friction later. However, while Queen's internal chemistry evolved, the essential dynamic stayed the same from their 1973 debut album to Mercury's death in 1991. There were certainly heated discussions and arguments during that time, but what went on within the group stayed within the group.

*'I won't be a rock star. I will be a legend.'*

*Freddie Mercury*

'WE CONSTANTLY HEAR ABOUT WHAT KIND OF A GREAT SHOWMAN FREDDIE WAS. AND SOMETIMES IT INFURIATES ME. NO, HE WAS NOT A SHOWMAN – HE WAS A GREAT MUSICIAN.'

ROGER TAYLOR

## Record Sales

As is the case for most of the world's biggest rock stars, trying to calculate Queen's record sales is difficult. The band have certified record sales around the world for 104 million, but most estimates of their actual sales are about twice that. That puts them comfortably in the Top 20 bestselling rock acts in the world – probably close to the Top 10.

Most significantly, Queen's *Greatest Hits* (1981) is the UK's biggest-selling album, with sales passing 6 million (meaning one in four British households now owns a copy!) and overtaking the Beatles' *Sgt. Pepper's Lonely Hearts Club Band* (1967). Further down the list of top bestselling UK albums, at No. 10 you'll find Queen's *Greatest Hits II* (1991). Queen's first *Greatest Hits* album accounts for nearly a third of their total UK sales and a quarter of their global sales.

Around half of Queen's worldwide sales come from outside Britain and the USA; this is a higher proportion than that of many of their peers, which makes them a truly global rock band.

*'Freddie is great. At a time when everybody else was doing God knows what, Freddie was making music.'*

*Ozzy Osbourne*

## Awards

Queen have been awarded two of the highest honours that the record industry can bestow: the Outstanding Contribution to British Music at the annual BRIT Awards in 1990 and an induction into the American Rock and Roll Hall of Fame in 2001.

However, the awards that Queen have always prized most highly are those voted by the public, dating back to 1974 when they were 2nd Most Promising New Name in British rock weekly *NME*'s annual poll. A year later, rival rock weekly *Melody Maker* made them Band of the Year, and by 1977, their fame had broadened, winning Best Group in a *Daily Mail* poll.

Queen's first world tour brought immediate international acclaim, with readers of Japan's *Music Life* going particularly Queen-crazy and voting them Top Group, Top Album, Top Single, Top Singer, Top Guitarist, Top Drummer and Top Bass Player in 1979. American rock fans were slightly more restrained, voting Queen 2nd Best Group in *Circus* magazine but awarding them Best Live Show. It was the same story after their pioneering South American tour in 1981 and their legendary Live Aid appearance in 1985.

*'The reason we're successful, darling?*
*My overall charisma, of course.'*

*Freddie Mercury*

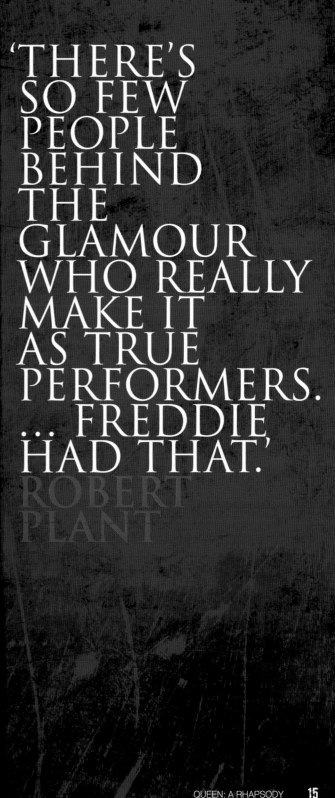

'THERE'S SO FEW PEOPLE BEHIND THE GLAMOUR WHO REALLY MAKE IT AS TRUE PERFORMERS. ... FREDDIE HAD THAT.'
ROBERT PLANT

# THE COMPLETE PACKAGE

'OF ALL THE MORE THEATRICAL ROCK PERFORMERS, FREDDIE TOOK IT FURTHER THAN THE REST. HE TOOK IT OVER THE EDGE.'
DAVID BOWIE

Queen's reputation rests squarely on their extraordinary sequence of hit singles through the 1970s and 1980s, which include 25 Top 10 hits, seven of which got to No. 1 with six more peaking at No. 2. Even more remarkable, though, is the range of styles they cover on their hits.

## Anthemic Songs

They wrote anthems ('We Are The Champions', 'We Will Rock You'), rockers ('Killer Queen', 'Hammer To Fall'), pop songs ('A Kind Of Magic', 'I Want To Break Free'), grandiose ('Innuendo', 'Somebody To Love') and quirky ('Crazy Little Thing Called Love', 'Under Pressure'). Or, as in the case of 'Bohemian Rhapsody', they just piled all the above styles into one glorious epic.

Whatever style they chose, they always superimposed it with their own identity, which means that you always know when you're listening to a Queen song. It's also what enabled them to maintain a seamless array of hits across two decades of constantly changing fashions and technical innovations.

## Albums

The success of Queen's *Greatest Hits* (1981) and *Greatest Hits II* (1991) has distracted attention from their 18 other albums released between 1973 and 1995. These albums chart the progress of the band more accurately than their dizzying array of hits. Both fans and critics generally agree that Queen's fourth album, *A Night At The Opera* (1975), is their finest. At the time, it was an awe-inspiring technical breakthrough – and not just because of 'Bohemian Rhapsody'. Nearly 40 years later, many of those innovations may sound primitive, but the exuberant vitality remains. *News Of The World*, released two years later, is Queen's most defiant album, from the knockout opening combination of 'We Will Rock You' and 'We Are The Champions' to May pre-empting Eddie Van Halen's guitar style on 'It's Late'. Meanwhile, *The Game* (1980) finds Queen at the peak of their powers, supremely confident with any style they choose.

*'I like people to go away from a Queen show feeling fully entertained, having had a good time.'*

*Freddie Mercury*

# 'THE WORST DAY OF MY LIFE WAS ONCE THAT MY MOM DIDN'T ALLOW ME TO GO TO A QUEEN CONCERT BECAUSE I WAS GROUNDED.'

## LARS ULRICH (METALLICA)

## Videos

From the beginning, Queen have always been aware that their image was crucial when it came to selling their music. The pioneering video they filmed for 'Bohemian Rhapsody' in 1975 is often reckoned to mark the dawn of the era of the pop promo.

And if their music had a twinkle, then their videos generally featured a sly wink at the camera – sometimes literally, always metaphorically and invariably innovative. Look at their homage to the *Metropolis* silent movie classic for 'Radio Ga Ga' and the synchronized handclaps, faithfully reproduced by the real audience at Live Aid. Another example is their young doppelgängers stealing the show from them on 'The Miracle', or the way the band morph from their 'Bohemian Rhapsody' video to themselves a decade later for 'One Vision'.

They weren't afraid to push boundaries, either: from Mercury's camp rockabilly for 'Crazy Little Thing Called Love' to the gloriously politically incorrect nude 'Bicycle Race'. And who can forget Queen in drag for 'I Want To Break Free', with Taylor's disturbingly realistic schoolgirl and Mercury hoovering away in his black leather miniskirt, complete with moustache? Actually, America can't even remember: not one TV channel dared to show it.

*'I only saw him (Freddie) in concert once and, as they say, he was definitely a man who could hold an audience in the palm of his hand.'*

*David Bowie*

## Live

Queen were a live band two years before they released a record. They started in sweaty dumps, learning how to work a crowd at close quarters and control their sound however loud they played – and they always played loud.

As soon as they progressed to dance halls and theatres, they upgraded their show (and their volume). Even before their Bohemian breakthrough, they were a sellout attraction across the UK, erupting onstage in a blaze of lights as the audience surged forward, leaving a trail of broken seats in their wake.

As the venues got bigger, so the lights and the special effects improved. The band mastered the art of playing their more complex songs live, using whatever technology was available. The trick was to dominate every stage they played on – from club to stadium. Their motto was: 'Blind 'em and deafen 'em.'

*'I think Queen songs are pure escapism... after that, they can go away and say that was great, and go back to their problems.'*

*Freddie Mercury*

# STYLE

'FREDDIE, IF YOU'RE OUT THERE AND YOU WANT TO CHOOSE ANY ARTIST TO CHANNEL YOUR WORK, PLEASE GIVE ME AN ALBUM, OR AT LEAST A MIDDLE EIGHT.'
ROBBIE WILLIAMS

**Q**ueen's style has always been varied, but it's nevertheless instantly identifiable; you know when you're listening to a Queen song. Their early albums straddled the line between heavy metal and glam rock with multitracked vocals, harmonies and intricate overdubbed guitars – but no synthesizers, as every album they released in the 1970s defiantly proclaimed. Every sound you think is a synthesizer actually comes from May's home-made guitar.

## Albums

With *A Night At The Opera* (1975), Queen started experimenting with other styles and ideas. The hits began to flow in earnest as their confidence grew. By the time *The Game* (1980) was released, they could encompass disco ('Another One Bites The Dust') and rockabilly ('Crazy Little

Thing Called Love') on the same album. Disco was a rare, unpopular move by the band and they returned to rock, reinvigorated, in the mid-1980s with fewer constraints than before. The final Queen albums have an indefinably intense but liberating quality that's impossible in retrospect to separate from Mercury's tragic decline and demise.

## Fourplay

One crucial factor that set Queen apart from all other major rock acts is that each member of the band was a multi-instrumentalist. All four of them also wrote songs – and not just songs, but big hits. Moreover, it's not as if each of them tended to write a particular kind of song. A breakdown of who wrote what in Queen shows that their individual styles were as varied as the band's style, and this gave them a unique dynamic.

Mercury wrote 'Bohemian Rhapsody', 'Somebody To Love' and 'We Are The Champions'; May wrote 'Fat Bottomed Girls', 'We Will Rock You' and 'Who Wants To Live Forever'; Deacon wrote 'Another One Bites The Dust', 'I Want To Break Free' and 'You're My Best Friend'; finally, Taylor wrote 'Radio Ga Ga', 'A Kind Of Magic' and 'These Are The Days Of Our Lives'.

## Fans

Queen fans are acknowledged as being amongst the most dedicated and loyal of any rock group. This has nothing to do with any media hype around the band – indeed, the press have frequently been critical of them – but is based on Queen's music and their different personalities. In fact, it often seemed that the

> 'THE BEST
> BAND
> IN THE
> WORLD
> IS QUEEN.
> DEFINITELY.'
> MATTHEW
> BELLAMY
> (MUSE)

more criticism they received in the press, the stronger their fan support became.

While fans of rock acts like U2 and Bruce Springsteen are frequently loud and voluble in acclaiming their heroes, Queen fans tended to be less demonstrative but quietly stronger in their support. This is not to say that Queen shows were quiet affairs – far from it. In the late 1980s, when the media became obsessed with Mercury's failing health, expecting his fans to be shocked by details of his hedonistic lifestyle, it became clear that most Queen fans were not interested in his lifestyle: they were just concerned about his health.

## Influence

Queen's own influences were broad, so it's scarcely surprising that the acts they influenced should be even more varied. The list of some of the guest stars who appeared at the Freddie Mercury Tribute Concert gives an indication of the variety: Metallica, Def Leppard, Guns N' Roses, Roger Daltrey, Tony Iommi, Robert Plant, Zucchero, Seal, Lisa Stansfield, David Bowie, Ian Hunter, Annie Lennox, George Michael, Elton John.

Other acts who freely acknowledge Queen's influence are even more diverse, and include Nirvana, Extreme, Foo Fighters, Green Day, Radiohead, Franz Ferdinand, Iron Maiden, Journey, Kansas, Katy Perry, Lady Gaga, Manic Street Preachers, Meat Loaf, Muse, Mötley Crüe, Van Halen, Smashing Pumpkins, Flaming Lips, Trent Reznor, My Chemical Romance, Robbie Williams, Queensrÿche, Styx, Steve Vai, the Killers and Panic! At The Disco.

'WE TOURED WITH QUEEN ON THEIR FIRST VISIT TO THE STATES AND BECAME GOOD FRIENDS. THEY PROFOUNDLY INFLUENCED US.'
KERRY LIVGREN (KANSAS)

# ONE VISION

'I GO THROUGH MAJOR CRISES EVERY FEW MONTHS, BUT THEN I HAVE GREAT PEAKS OF BELIEF AND CREATIVITY. I'M A WEIRD KIND OF ANIMAL.'
BRIAN MAY

The Queen story starts with Brian May. He was academically and technically smart, adapting his first acoustic guitar to an electric one and amplifying it through the radio on which he used to listen to pop music. With his father, he made a telescope and then a proper electric guitar, using motorbike valve springs to get tension on the strings and a saddlebag support frame for a tremolo arm. He called it the Red Special and has played it on every Queen album.

## Brian May

Brian May (born on 19 July 1947) grew up in the middle-class suburb of Feltham in West London. At Hampton Grammar School, he formed various bands that seldom got beyond rehearsing and changing line-ups, until he met fellow pupil and

# 'I PICKED UP A GUITAR AND FOUND IT VERY DIFFICULT AND I SORT OF GRADUATED TO DRUMS BECAUSE I FOUND THEM VERY EASY.'
## ROGER TAYLOR

singer Tim Staffell. Their band, 1984, played their first gig in 1964 and continued after May went to Imperial College London to study physics and astronomy. 1984 notably supported Jimi Hendrix at a college gig, before May left in early 1968 to focus on his final exams.

Even before taking his exams, May regretted leaving 1984 (which had since disintegrated), and he teamed up with Staffell again to form another group. They advertised for a 'Mitch Mitchell/Ginger Baker-style drummer', and among those who replied was a certain Roger Taylor....

## Roger Taylor

Roger Meddows-Taylor was born on 26 July 1949 in Norfolk and moved to Cornwall with his parents aged eight. From his early teens, he was desperate to be a musician, and his decision to study dentistry at the London Hospital Medical College was partly motivated by a desire to get closer to London's pop scene. His first band, Reaction, had just broken up when a friend told him about May's advertisement.

The three of them hit it off immediately and called their band Smile, playing their first gig at Imperial College, where they supported Pink Floyd. They built up a following on the London circuit, but made the mistake of signing to the American Mercury record label, which released one single in the US that bombed and then dropped them. Disheartened, Staffell quit in the spring of 1970, asking his flatmate if he might be interested in taking over. May and Taylor had already met Freddie....

## Freddie Mercury

Farrokh Bulsara was born on 5 September 1946 in Zanzibar (now part of Tanzania). His parents were Parsee Indians and he went to a boarding school near Bombay (Mumbai), where he was nicknamed Freddie. In 1964, with growing civil unrest in Zanzibar, the family emigrated to England, settling in Feltham (less than a mile away from May). Freddie's colonial education made the transition easy for him, and in 1966 he started a graphic illustration course at Ealing College of Art, where he met fellow student Tim Staffell.

Staffell taught Freddie some guitar chords and took him to some Smile gigs, inspiring Freddie to start his singing career. In 1969, he joined Liverpool trio Ibex who'd moved down to London. That didn't work out, and neither did spells with Sour Sea Milk and Wreckage. However, Freddie had discovered that he was a natural frontman and was adopting the persona of Freddie Mercury, who was determined to be a star. He was also running a stall in Kensington Market, selling Victorian clothes to fund his persona, helped by Taylor.

When Staffell quit Smile, May and Taylor were flummoxed and unsure whether to continue. It was Mercury who reinvigorated them with a stream of ideas about their music and presentation. The three of them decided to give it a go and Mercury came up with a new name, Queen. Throughout 1970, they wrote and rehearsed together, playing a few gigs with a handful of temporary bass players. They needed someone permanent, though.

'WE ARE PEOPLE NOT ANDROIDS. WE'VE GOT VIEWS....I THINK MUSIC IS ONE OF THE MOST POWERFUL MEDIA FORCES IN THE WORLD TODAY.'

ROGER TAYLOR

## John Deacon

John Richard Deacon was born in Leicester on 19 August 1951. Like May, he was technically and academically clever and, like May, built instruments with his father – in Deacon's case, a ham radio. His father died when he was 11, which was a traumatic blow, but he pursued an academic career at grammar school before going to Chelsea College in London in 1969, where he studied electronics and got a first-class honours degree.

He'd actually seen a Queen gig, but wasn't convinced until he was introduced to them by a mutual friend early in 1971. However, they gelled as soon as they started playing together, despite – or maybe because of – the fact that he was as introverted as Mercury was extroverted. Queen was now complete, and in order to celebrate, Mercury designed the now-famous Queen , which incorporates their astrological birth signs.

'Performing was how I dealt with my own insignificance. [...] I felt awkward because I was taller than my friends, too thin, had spots, didn't like my nose [...] , was petrified of dances because I couldn't communicate with girls. The easiest way out was to go on stage and play.'

Brian May

# GLAM
# ROCKERS

WE'VE GONE
OVERBOARD
ON EVERY
QUEEN ALBUM.
BUT THAT'S
QUEEN.'
FREDDIE
MERCURY

**Q**ueen may have come together in February 1971, but progress was painfully slow, mainly because they had to tend to their day jobs/postgraduate studies. It was five months before they played their first gig, but, on the plus side, that gave them plenty of time to sort their ideas out. And then they got two vital breaks. The first came when they were picked to test and demonstrate the recording facilities at the newly opened De Lane Lea studios in Wembley, North London, to potential clients. In return, they were given studio time to record their own demos.

## Keeping Themselves Alive

Their second break arrived when young producers John Anthony and Roy Thomas Baker visited the studio and were

# 'SHE'S A KILLER QUEEN. GUNPOWDER, GELATINE, DYNAMITE WITH A LASER BEAM. GUARANTEED TO BLOW YOUR MIND. ANYTIME.'

## 'KILLER QUEEN'

more impressed with Queen running through 'Keep Yourself Alive' than they were with the facilities. They were staff producers at Trident Studios and their bosses were looking to expand into band management.

Queen agreed a recording, management and publishing deal with Trident in the summer of 1972 that gave them access to the 24-track studio whenever it was not in use, which meant some pretty strange working hours. By the end of the year, they'd made their first album and, after the tapes were hawked around, they were eventually signed to EMI.

Their first single, the vibrant 'Keep Yourself Alive', was released in July 1973, with a promotional blitz that backfired when Radio 1 became suspicious of the hype and refused to playlist it. Their self-titled album – predominantly hard rock with elements of glam, folk-rock and jazz – showed their prowess and potential. It didn't quite make the Top 20, but it sold steadily everywhere they played that year, which included a support slot on Mott The Hoople's 20-date UK tour. Even though they were still getting their image together – at one point experimenting with a monochrome look (right down to their fingernails) – they'd already learnt how to make an impact.

## Procession

The band started recording their second album just weeks after releasing their first. This time, they were given 'proper' studio time at Trident and they made full use of it. The album was finished quite quickly, but put on hold while they continued promoting their first one.

'IN THE
EARLY DAYS,
WE JUST
WORE BLACK
ON STAGE.
VERY BOLD,
MY DEAR.
THEN WE
INTRODUCED
WHITE, FOR
VARIETY,
AND
IT SIMPLY
GREW
AND GREW.'
FREDDIE
MERCURY

# RAPTUROUS RHAPSODY

'THERE WASN'T
MUCH SEX AND
DRUGS ... WELL,
THERE WASN'T
MUCH DRUGS!'
ROGER TAYLOR

In 1975, Queen managed to break out of their cult band status. They spent six months touring three continents: they sparked mayhem across the UK and Europe – where Sheer Heart Attack (1974) and 'Killer Queen' went Top 10 in most countries – cracked the lucrative Japanese market and made good progress in the US (where the album and single both reached No. 12), until Mercury's voice packed up.

## A New Start

However, when they returned home, it was to their squalid, damp-infested single-room flats in London – and no money, even when they asked. Disillusioned and increasingly bitter, they hired lawyers to extricate themselves from their Trident deal and set about finding new management. After some deliberation, they chose Elton John's manager, John Reid.

'I HAVE TO WIN PEOPLE OVER. [...] THAT'S PART OF MY DUTY. IT'S ALL TO DO WITH FEELING IN CONTROL.'
FREDDIE MERCURY

'WE'RE A VERY EXPENSIVE GROUP; WE BREAK A LOT OF RULES. IT'S UNHEARD OF TO COMBINE OPERA WITH A ROCK THEME, MY DEAR.'

FREDDIE MERCURY

By August they were ready to start recording their fourth album, and they gathered at Rockfield Studios in Wales to go through their individual contributions.

## Bismillah

Mercury had been working on 'Bohemian Rhapsody' for some five years before he brought it to the band. It veered from ballad to heavy metal to 'mock' opera, with a cappella vocals and a riot of lyrical references. It was a huge challenge to record for the band and producer Roy Thomas Baker, not least because of the 180 vocal overdubs that literally wore out the master tape.

As the album's *pièce de résistance*, it was the obvious choice for a single, but, at a few seconds under six minutes, it was far too long to get radio airplay. EMI refused to release it and Queen refused to edit it. The impasse was solved when a copy was slipped to DJ Kenny Everett at London's Capital Radio, who played it 14 times over a weekend. On the Monday, London record shops were inundated with requests for the single. It was rush-released on 31 October 1975 and spent nine weeks at No. 1 before passing into legend. When it was re-released in 1991, it became the first single to sell a million copies twice. It currently ranks as the all-time third-biggest selling single in Britain, behind Elton John's 'Candle In The Wind' and Band Aid's 'Do They Know It's Christmas?'.

## Good Company

The success of 'Bohemian Rhapsody' tends to overshadow the album it came from: *A Night At The Opera* (1975) is a

# 'IN THE QUIET OF THE NIGHT LET OUR CANDLE ALWAYS BURN, LET US NEVER LOSE THE LESSONS WE HAVE LEARNED.'

## 'TEO TORRIATTE (LET US CLING TOGETHER)'

glittering array of Queen's individual and collective talents. Each member of the group wrote at least one fine song. In addition to Mercury's magnum opus, May came up with the equally grandiose eight-minute 'The Prophets Song', Taylor set his inner boy racer free on 'I'm In Love With My Car', and Deacon came up with the deceptively simple but genial 'You're My Best Friend', the album's other Top 10 single.

From the coruscating opener 'Death On Two Legs (Dedicated To…)' – which had their former Trident bosses foaming at the mouth until they were financially sedated – to the final Hendrix-inspired 'God Save The Queen', the album's production pushes the technical limits, sometimes mesmerizingly so. It was Queen's most pop album so far, and, arguably, their best.

## Teo Torriatte

Not surprisingly, success and fame changed Queen. For a start, they could afford decent houses. May and Deacon had married their girlfriends, but Mercury ended his five-year relationship with Mary Austin and started going out with boys.

There was a whiff of 'follow-up' about A Day At The Races, released in December 1976 – and not just because they'd nicked another Marx Brothers movie title. For the first time, they produced themselves, and the result was style over substance. That didn't stop it going to No. 1, though. Another lengthy world tour hadn't left them enough time to come up with the songs. Although the first single ('Somebody To Love') marched to No. 2, the second ('Tie Your Mother Down') failed to make the Top 30, which was something of a jolt for the band.

# WE WILL
# ROCK YOU

'A CONCERT IS
NOT A LIVE
RENDITION
OF OUR
ALBUM. IT'S
A THEATRICAL
EVENT.'
FREDDIE
MERCURY

By 1977, the 'Bohemian Rhapsody' effect had spread around the world and Queen took their increasingly grandiose show across North America. They now had a two-ton lighting rig in the shape of a crown that rose up behind the stage above a sea of dry ice. Mercury was the icing on the cake, however, stretching his flamboyance to diva-esque extremes: toasting the audience with champagne, tossing them carnations or (de-thorned) roses, and strutting the stage in tight satin shorts and a kimono. 'I'm into the ballet thing,' he gaily proclaimed.

## If You Can't Beat Them

Back home, Queen's preening style was a target for the growing punk movement and critics labelled their rock opulence 'grotesque'. The contrast was vividly apparent on the night of Her

Majesty's Jubilee celebrations, when Queen were completing four nights at Wembley Arena while the Sex Pistols were being arrested for having a noisy boat party on the River Thames.

Queen decided that their next album would be less produced and more spontaneous, and booked the workmanlike Wessex Studios in London. Imagine their surprise when they found the Sex Pistols working in the next studio. There was good-natured banter between Mercury and Sid Vicious – or Sid Ferocious, as Mercury called him. Some of it rubbed off, too. Taylor's 'Sheer Heart Attack' (lying around unfinished since the album of the same name) and May's 'It's Late' both had a new-wave gusto about them.

However, it was the two anthems that opened *News Of The World* (1977) that raised Queen to another level. May's 'We Will Rock You' was inspired by crowd chants between songs at a gig, and was driven by foot stomps and handclaps instead of drums. On the other hand, Mercury's 'We Are The Champions' was a deliberate attempt to write a football-crowd-style sing-along for Queen's own crowd. Released together as a double A-sided single, it failed to top the charts in the UK and US but hung around them for months, seeping into the wider public consciousness around the world.

## Bottoms And Bicycles

Before their next tour, Queen reorganized their business affairs, parting company with John Reid (who was finding it impossible to manage both Elton John and Queen) and restructuring their whole operation. Their new accountant advised them to

> 'FROM THE BEGINNING OF QUEEN THERE WAS SUCH MOMENTUM THAT I NEVER HAD ANY TIME TO DO ANYTHING ELSE. MY ENERGY WAS 95% FOCUSED ON THE BAND.'
> BRIAN MAY

become tax exiles for a year and they recorded their *Jazz* album (1978) in Switzerland and France.

Despite reuniting with producer Roy Thomas Baker, the album failed to gel, mainly because of the uneven material. Nevertheless, the best songs had a special zing: the hedonistic 'Don't Stop Me Now' and the ribald cartoon duo of 'Fat Bottomed Girls' and 'Bicycle Race' that was released as a double A-side. The 'Bicycle Race' video, which showed 63 naked girls (variously bottomed) riding bikes around Wimbledon Stadium, caused controversy wherever it was shown. The debauched album launch party in New Orleans was another exercise in excess.

## Killing You Loudly

The tours of Europe and Japan that followed the *Jazz* album in late 1978 were recorded for a live album. Unfortunately, they picked the wrong tour. The band were sounding jaded, as the treadmill of album and tour was beginning to take its toll. The show was loud and frenetic, but the *joie de vivre* they had displayed previously was missing. Although the band had developed ingenious ways of performing their complicated songs onstage, without the lights and visual effects, these attempts still paled in comparison to the studio versions. In particular, you couldn't see Mercury's new leather-clad look.

Worse still, they left in 'Bohemian Rhapsody', which used backing tapes, as it was impossible to reproduce live. The band even exited the stage and left the video running. Not that any of this prevented *Live Killers* from charting at No. 3 when it was released in June 1979.

'PEOPLE WANT ART. THEY WANT SHOWBIZ. THEY WANT TO SEE YOU RUSH OFF IN YOUR LIMOUSINE.'
FREDDIE MERCURY

# CRAZY LITTLE THINGS

'WE'RE A BIT
FLASHY, BUT
THE MUSIC'S
NOT ONE
BIG NOISE.'
FREDDIE
MERCURY

**B**y 1979, Queen had been together long enough to start getting on each other's nerves, especially when it came to the studio. However, this produced some unexpected results. That summer, they booked themselves into Musicland Studios in Munich. Sitting in his bath, Mercury wrote 'Crazy Little Thing Called Love' in 10 minutes. It was recorded that night, complete with a rockabilly guitar solo by a deeply suspicious May. In early 1980, it became Queen's first US No. 1, topping the charts for four weeks.

## Game On

Then Deacon, a closet Chic fan, unveiled 'Another One Bites The Dust', and this time, it was Taylor who threw a hissy fit, commenting, 'This isn't rock'n'roll. What the hell are we

# 'THERE'S SOMETHING RATHER NICE ABOUT SPENDING THE EVENING HITTING THINGS.'
## ROGER TAYLOR

doing?' He even had to muffle his drums while backwards piano, cymbal crashes, handclaps and guitar flourishes were added with producer Reinhold Mack. It was the antithesis of the way Queen normally worked, but it gave them their second US No. 1 and was a chart-topper for three weeks.

Bolstered by two No. 1 hits, *The Game* (1980) was Queen's first US album chart-topper – for five weeks. They were now selling out three nights at New York's Madison Square Garden and Mercury was making an entrance on the shoulders of a Darth Vader-clad roadie – until *Star Wars* producer George Lucas displayed his own sense of humour by putting a stop to it.

Mercury also got further into 'this ballet thing' when he made a guest appearance with the London Ballet Company at a gala charity show, performing a strenuously rehearsed routine to 'Bohemian Rhapsody' and 'Crazy Little Thing Called Love'.

The band broke new territory, too, writing the soundtrack to the *Flash Gordon* movie that got better reviews than the film itself. In February 1981, they were the first major band to tour South America, transporting 60 tons of equipment and building their own stages to play stadium shows to some 350,000 people in Argentina (where their albums occupied the entire Top 10) and Brazil. The expenses were huge, but so was the gross: nearly £2 million. However, when they tried to repeat the exercise later that year in Venezuela and Mexico, they got caught up in an orgy of corruption and were lucky to escape with their gear and a half a million pounds loss.

## Heat And Pressure

Between their South American adventures, Queen spent the summer at their own Mountain Studios in Switzerland, and when David Bowie arrived to work on some recordings, a studio hook-up was engineered. Sparks and other combustibles flew, and 24 hours later, they were recording 'Under Pressure'. The fact that any of that spontaneity survived the diva dramatics during the mixing sessions – and the final mix was a dog's dinner – was a miracle. However, the British public believed and it topped the charts in late 1981, although the Americans were more sceptical and it barely made the Top 30 there. Still, it was all good publicity for Queen's *Greatest Hits* (1981).

Back in Munich and Musicland, Queen let their love of the local nightlife and disco clubs spill over into their next album, *Hot Space* (1982). Mercury's 'Body Language' had funk and synthesizers and the album's opener, 'Staying Power', featured a horn arrangement by Aretha Franklin's arranger. Only May was keeping the hard rock faith with 'Dancer' and 'Put Out The Fire'. 'Body Language' was a bigger hit in the US than in the UK, despite MTV banning the video because of the amount of bare skin on display. But the Americans were cool on the album, and they were even cooler on Mercury's 'gay' moustache. Queen's 1982 US tour would be their last.

*'The lavish presentation appeals to me, and I've got to convince the others.'*

*Freddie Mercury*

## Going Ga Ga

Wisely, Queen took 1983 off. They were in danger of stalling – as a band and individually. They did solo projects (Mercury did some never-released songs with Michael Jackson, whereas May played the blues with Eddie Van Halen) and then came back together reinvigorated. Each of them wrote a hit on *The Works* (1984): Taylor's anthemic 'Radio Ga Ga', Deacon's simple pop song 'I Want To Break Free', May's heavy riff-laden 'Hammer To Fall' and Mercury's emotive 'It's A Hard Life'. However, in the US, the hits dried up after 'Radio Ga Ga' and the album stopped short of the Top 20.

Queen geared up for their live show – and then they walked into trouble. Sun City, an exclusive resort in South Africa, was a symbol of the apartheid regime. In vain did the band protest that they played to unsegregated audiences and that they were free to express their anti-apartheid views: Sun City was on a United Nations cultural blacklist that Queen deliberately ignored. They were universally condemned, although when the African National Congress adopted 'I Want To Break Free' in the late 1980s, it provided an ironic twist to the tale.

*'Don't stop me now,*
*I'm having such a good time.*
*I'm having a ball.'*

*'Don't Stop Me Now'*

'PLAYING WITH QUEEN WAS THE BIGGEST MOMENT OF MY CAREER. IT WAS LIKE LIVING A CHILDHOOD FANTASY.'
GEORGE MICHAEL

# LIVE AID

'EACH GIG
SHOULD BE
UNIQUE.
YOU'RE ALWAYS
TREADING
THAT LINE
BETWEEN
KEEPING
YOURSELF
FRESH AND
GIVING PEOPLE
SOMETHING
THEY WANT
TO HEAR.'
BRIAN MAY

For their Works tour of Europe and the UK, Queen's stage featured a couple of giant rotating cogs, echoing the Metropolis theme of the 'Radio Ga Ga' video, and they made a point of emphasizing their heavier songs. Mercury was placated with a specially designed catwalk on which to parade, and he was now channelling his disco infatuation into his solo album, Mr. Bad Guy (1985).

## Rock In Rio

Early in 1985, Queen returned to South America to open and close the Rock in Rio Festival, in Brazil. A total of 600,000 people watched their two shows that romped through their greatest hits. The only tricky moment came when Mercury donned his black leather miniskirt to sing 'I Want To Break Free' and was assailed by cans and bottles by the audience who thought he was mocking a song that had a particular social and political meaning for them. Hurriedly realizing his mistake, Mercury changed back and returned draped in a double-sided flag with the Union Jack on one side and the green and gold of Brazil on the other.

## Live Aid Invitation

After the gargantuan Rock in Rio Festival, Queen found it hard to get motivated for their stadium tour of Australia. Unwilling to rebuild their US popularity by intensive touring, they began eyeing other potential markets, such as Russia and Eastern Europe.

Then Bob Geldof got in touch to persuade them to play the Live Aid concert he was putting together to help Ethiopian famine victims. At this point, the show was still in the planning stages, but Geldof was particularly interested in Queen, as he wanted a band with international appeal to attract live worldwide TV coverage. He offered them a late afternoon spot with the biggest potential audience across the globe: 20 minutes, no sound check, no lights and no special effects – and no money, obviously. After some deliberation, the band agreed and started working out how to maximize the limited time they had been given.

## The Perfect Show

Soon after 6 pm on a warm 13 July 1985, Queen bounded onstage to a rapturous welcome. Mercury, 'dressed down' in stonewashed jeans and a white singlet, headed to the grand piano and tinkered with a few chords to get the volume right before playing the opening sequence of 'Bohemian Rhapsody'. The crowd, who were effectively a Queen audience, already had

# "I WENT OUTSIDE AND I HEARD THIS SOUND AND I THOUGHT, GOD, WHO'S GOT THEIR SOUND TOGETHER?", AND IT WAS QUEEN. THE CROWD WAS GOING CRAZY.'

**BOB GELDOF**

their hands aloft before the band switched to 'Radio Ga Ga', with the audience clapping in perfect unison. After indulging in some 'Eeayo' call-and-response antics, the band stormed into 'Hammer To Fall' and then sashayed their way through 'Crazy Little Thing Called Love' that Mercury dedicated to 'only the beautiful people here tonight – which means all of you'.

Rising above the applause, the primal stomp of 'We Will Rock You' produced another sea of raised arms across the stadium that turned into swaying waves with 'We Are The Champions' and ended with Queen's well-practised tumultuous finale. They took their bows and left, having broken their curfew by nearly a minute.

## The World They Created

By common consent, Queen stole the star-studded show at Live Aid. They understood the 'global jukebox' nature of the event and they had rehearsed for it. Their 20-minute set – six songs, every one of them a worldwide hit – has been hailed as the finest rock performance ever. Despite their meticulous preparations, the show was unhurried and relaxed. What they delivered was the very essence of Queen.

Such was the impact of Queen's show – immediately acknowledged by their fellow stars – that Mercury and May's subsequent appearance for an acoustic version of 'Is This The World We Created…?' from *The Works* (1984) album passed almost unnoticed. The song, which had been written after the pair had watched a TV documentary on poverty in Africa, was played at Live Aid while the stage was being set for Paul McCartney and the grand finale of the concert.

'[QUEEN] WERE ABSOLUTELY THE BEST BAND OF THE DAY. THEY PLAYED THE BEST, THEY HAD THE BEST SOUND, THEY USED THEIR SEVENTEEN MINUTES OR WHATEVER TO THE BEST ADVANTAGE.'
BOB GELDOF

# IT'S MAGIC

'FOR ME, FREDDIE IS THE BRIGHTEST REPRESENTATIVE OF THE ERA OF ROCK, WHEN PEOPLE WERE NOT AFRAID TO LIVE LIFE TO THE FULL. THIS WOULD HARDLY EVER BE REPEATED.'
ANNIE LENNOX

When Queen regrouped in Munich in the autumn of 1985, the Live Aid feel-good factor was still in the air. Film director Russell Mulcahy had persuaded the band to write the soundtrack for his Highlander movie, but they got temporarily diverted when Taylor came in with 'One Vision', inspired by Martin Luther King's 'I had a dream…' speech. By the time the rest of the group had finished with it (the first song that was collectively credited to Queen), 'One Vision' had a more general peace-and-love theme.

## The Magic Of Highlander

Released in November 1985, 'One Vision' was Queen's first post-Live Aid single and a UK Top 10, although there were accusations of cashing in on Live Aid that revived lingering resentment at their Sun City escapade. There was no mention

of the proceeds of 'Is This The World We Created…?' going to a Soweto educational charity.

Through the autumn of 1985 and the spring of 1986, Queen worked in the studio, first recording the soundtrack for the *Highlander* movie and then reworking several of the songs for their own album. These included May's grand 'Who Wants To Live Forever?', which echoed the theme of the film, and Taylor's 'A Kind Of Magic', inspired by a line in the film script and reworked by Mercury to turn it into a pop song.

Not only were the band working in different combinations that freshened up their music – Mercury and Deacon teamed up for 'Friends Will Be Friends' – but they were also recording with outsiders: composer Michael Kamen who arranged orchestral parts, their touring keyboard player Spike Edney, saxophonist Steve Gregory and Joan Armatrading on backing vocals. There were more special guests on *A Kind Of Magic* (1986) than on all of their previous albums.

## Retreat From Munich

Just like the band's previous two albums, *A Kind Of Magic* yielded four hit singles for Queen. However, this time, there was a sense that they had found a fruitful musical direction to pursue, rather than the disco rhythms that had been a divisive factor within the group, as well as confusing and alienating for some of their audience. Live Aid had indeed been a turning point for the band; they now knew what they did best as a band – and individually, they had their solo projects in which to indulge their own musical hobbies.

'I HAVE FUN WITH MY CLOTHES ONSTAGE; IT'S NOT A CONCERT YOU'RE SEEING, IT'S A FASHION SHOW.'
FREDDIE MERCURY

# 'I'M JUST A MUSICAL PROSTITUTE, MY DEAR.'
## FREDDIE MERCURY

*A Kind Of Magic* also marked the end of Queen's love affair with Munich and the Musicland Studio. The band had all enjoyed the city's hedonistic lifestyle, with its all-night clubs and discos – and none more so than Mercury. However, by the mid-1980s, the spectre of AIDS, which had first been noticed among the gay scene at the beginning of the decade, had changed that atmosphere irrevocably. At the end of 1985, Mercury sold his Munich apartment and moved to his refurbished house in Kensington.

## The Last Tour

In the summer of 1986, Queen set out on a 26-date stadium tour across Europe, taking their own 19.5-m (64-ft)-wide stage with two 12-m (40-ft) walkways on either side for Mercury's exclusive use (there were three stages 'leapfrogging' each other from city to city), 5,000 speakers, nine miles of cables and a huge video screen. The show opened with a sequence of songs from *A Kind Of Magic* and closed with their Live Aid set. For the finale, Mercury wore his most flamboyant outfit yet: a jewelled crown and red ermine-lined gown that trailed behind him.

In England, Queen filled football grounds in Newcastle and Manchester, and, just a year on from their Live Aid triumph, Wembley Stadium – twice. Such was the demand for tickets that another show – at Knebworth Park – was added at the end of the tour, after the band's first foray into Eastern Europe in Budapest, Hungary. The Knebworth show on 9 August – attended by in excess of 120,000 people – would be Queen's last show with Mercury.

'I DRESS
TO KILL,
BUT
TASTEFULLY.'
FREDDIE
MERCURY

# WAITING FOR A MIRACLE

'THE DIFFERENCE BETWEEN FREDDIE AND ALMOST ALL THE OTHER ROCK STARS WAS THAT HE WAS SELLING THE VOICE'
MONTSERRAT CABALLÉ

**A**fter Queen's Knebworth concert, Mercury told the others that he no longer wanted to tour. He later said in a radio interview that he wanted to break 'the cycle of album/tour/ album/tour'. He was also aware that, as he approached his fortieth birthday, he couldn't maintain his standard of performance indefinitely without becoming a parody of himself. Although there had always been an element of self-parody involved, this depended on his audience laughing with him rather than at him.

## Time Apart

The band decided to take a year off, but first, they compiled a live album from the summer tour that did full justice to their stage sound and made a powerful impact without the need for

visual effects. There were, however, complaints about the way some songs were edited in order to fit the album length – not that it stopped the album getting to No. 3 at the end of 1986.

During 1987, May and Taylor both immersed themselves in solo projects, partly as a distraction from their failing marriages. May played sessions with a host of artists, ranging from pop to metal, and produced songs for comedy heavy rock band Bad News and *EastEnders* actress Anita Dobson – who would become his second wife. Taylor formed his own band, The Cross, stepping out front to sing and play guitar. Their first video featured Cadbury's Flake model Debbie Leng – who would become his second wife. Deacon, on the other hand, kept his customary low profile.

Mercury, meanwhile, indulged his musical fantasies to the max. His wildly extravagant cover of The Platters' 1950s hit 'The Great Pretender' milked every drop of drama from the song, with Mercury singing all the backing vocals. The video was even more over-the-top, with Mercury in a dazzling suit sweeping down a staircase flanked by cardboard cut-outs of himself, reprising various roles in earlier Queen videos and getting back in drag with Roger Taylor. The single was a No. 4 hit in the spring of 1987.

## Mercury Rising And Falling

Mercury's next venture took him into the world of opera. On seeing Spanish soprano Montserrat Caballé perform at London's Royal Opera House, he was enraptured by her voice. Their friendship blossomed into an album of duets in which Mercury gave his operatic instincts full rein – nowhere more so

# 'THERE'S A RUMOUR GOING ROUND. I GOT A CLEAR OUTTA TOWN, YEAH I'M SMELLING LIKE A DRY FISH.'

## 'STONE COLD CRAZY'

than in the epic 'Barcelona', written in homage to Caballé's hometown and adopted as the city's theme song for the 1992 Olympics. Mercury, however, would not be attending….

In the spring of 1987 Mercury tested positive for HIV. He told only his closest friends – which did not include the other members of Queen to begin with – and plunged himself more deeply into his work. His woes were compounded when a former friend sold a kiss-and-tell story to a tabloid paper. Media speculation was intense, but Mercury flatly denied the rumours and the questions, and then decamped to Montreux to avoid the siege.

## (I Want It) All Together Now

Queen regrouped to record another album at the start of 1988, as planned. They took two decisions that would have an important impact on the music: all songs would be credited to Queen collectively rather than individually, and they would go back to recording together in the studio rather than separately. It brought them back together as a band. Each of them was dealing with personal issues – Mercury told the others about his illness but didn't want to talk about it – and the new working practices revived the band camaraderie.

The first song they worked on was a real Queen throwback: May's loudly defiant 'I Want It All'. It was the first of five hit singles from the No. 1 album *The Miracle* (1989). 'Breakthru', 'The Invisible Man', 'Scandal' and the album's title track all showed that the band's versatile rock/pop instincts were as sharp as ever. It took a year to make *The Miracle,* but they'd been productive, working on some 30 songs before making the final choice.

'I'M PRETTY BASIC AS FAR AS TECHNIQUE IS CONCERNED. I DON'T USE MANY GADGETS, AND I LIKE THE SOUND MY GUITAR MAKES, ANYWAY.'

BRIAN MAY

# WHO WANTS TO LIVE FOREVER?

'WHAT WILL I BE DOING IN TWENTY YEARS' TIME? I'LL BE DEAD, DARLING! ARE YOU CRAZY?'
FREDDIE MERCURY

As soon as they'd finished recording The Miracle (1989), Mercury urged the rest of the band back into the studio to work on new songs. Once they'd got over their surprise and understood why, the others willingly adapted their own lives to accommodate Mercury's work/rest programme, recording in bursts of two or three weeks and then working on their own projects while he rested.

## Innuendo And Rumour

Once again, they pooled songs and ideas, although it's usually possible to tell who wrote the original song, such as May's 'I Can't Live With You' and 'Headlong' or Mercury's 'Delilah' and 'All God's People'. 'Innuendo' unusually sprang out of an instrumental jam session at the Montreux Concert Hall that had Mercury scampering from the control room next door to join in.

May remembers the feeling of making the album 'on borrowed time', while Taylor said that it was 'a happy album to make'.

The recording of *Innuendo* (1991) was split between the calm serenity of Montreux and London, where Mercury could receive medical treatment but where he was also stalked by the paparazzi trying to catch him on a bad day. His health was fluctuating. At a TV recording in November 1989, he looked fit and healthy; three months later, receiving a BRIT Award for Queen's Outstanding Contribution to British Music, he looked gaunt and drawn.

To anyone outside the small circle of those who knew, there was a blanket denial to any rumours, and those who knew did not ask questions. Mercury was not discussing his condition; he was dealing with it in his own way. This left the rest of the band in the unenviable position of denying constantly that Mercury had AIDS while having to come up with excuses for his no-shows at interviews and promotional appearances. Fortunately, there were distractions to talk about, such as Vanilla Ice's sampling of 'Under Pressure' without permission for 'Ice Ice Baby'.

## The Days Of Their Lives

Beyond the media hounding, Queen's music continued to speak for itself. 'Innuendo', souped-up from the original jam into a six-and-a-half-minute extravaganza with Mercury wailing above May's guitar orchestra and Taylor's thrashing drums, was an unexpected No. 1 early in 1991. The *Innuendo* album (1991) did the same in March and even made a modest American showing at No. 30.

It was getting harder, though, to conceal what was really happening on video. The skilful animated effects of 'Innuendo' skirted round the problem, while the live 'Headlong' was shot on a good day, albeit in soft focus. Also, Mercury's face make-up that was supposed to echo the quirkiness of 'I'm Going Slightly Mad' looked more like a cover-up, even in black and white. Mercury's last video appearance in 'These Are The Days Of Our Lives' is, in retrospect, heart-rending to watch.

## Rain Must Fall

Still, Mercury wanted to carry on recording after *Innuendo*. Away from prying eyes, in Montreux, the sessions were now down to two or three days at a time before he needed to rest, but the others used the spare time to write and record demos for him to work on when he could. This continued through the first half of 1991 and included the last song that Mercury wrote, 'A Winter's Tale', and his last, remarkably powerful, vocal on 'Mother Love', for which he was apparently barely able to stand.

Arriving back in London in early November 1991, shortly after 'The Show Must Go On' was released, Mercury took a decision to stop taking the drugs for his illness. On 23 November, he issued a statement confirming that he had AIDS, adding that the reason for not disclosing the information earlier was 'to protect the privacy of those around me'. He died the following day.

*'If I had to do it all over again? Why not, I would do it a little bit differently.'*

*Freddie Mercury*

'WHEN WE LOST FREDDIE,' WE NOT ONLY LOST A GREAT PERSONALITY, A MAN WITH A GREAT SENSE OF HUMOUR, A TRUE SHOWMAN, BUT WE LOST PROBABLY THE BEST.'
ROGER DALTREY

'FREDDIE FILLED A VERY LARGE PART OF MY LIFE – THE LIFE OF THE OTHERS IN THE BAND – BUT MOST ESPECIALLY THE MILLIONS OF PEOPLE HE NEVER MET.'
ROGER TAYLOR

# FITTING MEMORIALS

'WHEN YOU'RE THROUGH WITH LIFE AND ALL HOPE IS LOST, HOLD OUT YOUR HAND COS FRIENDS WILL BE FRIENDS RIGHT TILL THE END.'

'FRIENDS WILL BE FRIENDS'

The day after Mercury's death, May, Taylor and Deacon issued their own statement expressing their loss and grief but also their pride 'in the courageous way that he lived and died'. They promised to celebrate his life 'in the style to which he was accustomed'. The tabloid media, which had been wrong-footed by Mercury's final statement, frantically fished for salacious details before realizing that they had misjudged the public mood. There was overwhelming affection and sympathy for Mercury and no interest in digging for dirt.

## Spreading Awareness

Not surprisingly, sales of Queen's albums increased substantially in the following weeks. 'The Show Must Go On' went back up the charts again and even Brian May's newly

'THE MORE
YOU LISTEN
TO QUEEN
THE MORE
YOU REALIZE,
ESPECIALLY
IF YOU'RE A
MUSICIAN,
HOW MUCH
OF A GENIUS
FREDDIE
MERCURY
WAS, AND
HOW MUCH
BRIAN MAY
AND THE
OTHER
GUYS ARE.'
KID ROCK

released solo single 'Driven By You' shot into the Top 10. Just before Christmas 1991, 'Bohemian Rhapsody' was re-released, coupled with 'These Are The Days Of Our Lives', going to No. 1, with proceeds of more than £1 million going to the Terrence Higgins Trust AIDS charity.

In February 1992, while collecting a special award for Mercury at the BRIT Awards, May and Taylor announced a tribute concert in April at Wembley Stadium to launch the Mercury Phoenix Trust AIDS charity. All 72,000 tickets sold out within six hours, before any of the acts had been confirmed.

The three remaining Queen members organized a show that featured British and American bands influenced by Queen in the first half, and then performed with a series of guest singers. The two outstanding moments came late on, with George Michael's superb cover of 'Somebody To Love' (a No. 1 when it was released a year later), followed by Elton John putting his own stamp on 'Bohemian Rhapsody', before a manic Axl Rose bounded onstage to drive the song to its conclusion. Rose and Guns N' Roses' inclusion in the show had attracted criticism because of the homophobic lyrics in the song 'One In A Million', but Rose and Elton John finished 'Bohemian Rhapsody' arm in arm in a practical demonstration of the concert's aim of AIDS awareness.

## Queenelicious

Queen's low profile in America meant that Mercury's death did not register there as strongly as it did around the rest of the world. However, the band received an unexpected boost in

# 'THERE IS ONLY ONE FREDDIE, AND IT IS IMPOSSIBLE TO REPLACE HIM.'
JOHN DEACON

the summer of 1992 thanks to the hit teen comedy movie *Wayne's World* and its opening sequence of four guys in a car singing and headbanging along to 'Bohemian Rhapsody'. The reissued single got to No. 2 in the US charts and raised $300,000 for the Magic Johnson AIDS Foundation.

Meanwhile, the three remaining Queen members declined to bring the band to a close, even though they all said that trying to replace Mercury would be 'wrong' and 'impossible'. After the tribute concert, Taylor and Deacon took an extended break, but May actively pushed his solo career, scoring a No. 5 UK hit with 'Too Much Love Will Kill You', and forming a band and touring Europe and America.

## Made In Heaven And Montreux

In the spring of 1994, Taylor and Deacon started working on Mercury's final vocal recordings, made after *Innuendo* (1991), adding instrumental parts to create songs. May joined them later, reworking the songs and broadening the project to include earlier incomplete pieces and tracks from Mercury's *Mr Bad Guy* (1985) solo album, for which they recorded new backing tracks.

Released in late 1995, *Made In Heaven* went straight to No. 1 in the UK and seven other European countries, although it failed to make the US Top 50. Five singles were taken from the album over the next year, including 'Heaven For Everyone' and 'A Winter's Tale' – Mercury's last song. The album cover featured the larger-than-life statue of Mercury by Czech sculptor Irena Sedlecká in the garden of his house overlooking Lake Geneva. The statue has since been moved to the lake shoreline in Montreux.

# THE BAND PLAYED ON

'THE GUITAR
WAS MY
WEAPON,
MY SHIELD TO
HIDE BEHIND.'
BRIAN MAY

After a gap of nearly five years, May, Taylor and Deacon appeared together with Elton John at the start of 1997 in Paris, performing 'The Show Must Go On' at the opening night of a new ballet, Ballet For Life. This was inspired in part by Mercury's battle against AIDS and featured 17 Queen songs and a dozen Mozart pieces. The trio also recorded a new song, 'No-One But You (Only The Good Die Young)', which was dedicated to Mercury and included on the Queen Rocks (1997) compilation later that year.

## Raising The Roof

It was Deacon's last contribution to the band before retiring, but May and Taylor were not prepared to let it lie. They pursued their respective solo careers, but always seemed to be on the lookout for another chance to revive the Queen legacy. The next

'YOU CAN BE ANYTHING YOU WANT TO BE. JUST TURN YOURSELF INTO ANYTHING YOU THINK THAT YOU COULD EVER BE.'
'INNUENDO'

'MY SOUL IS PAINTED LIKE THE WINGS OF BUTTERFLIES. FAIRY TALES OF YESTERDAY WILL GROW BUT NEVER DIE. I CAN FLY, MY FRIENDS.'
'THE SHOW MUST GO ON'

opportunity came in 2000, when they teamed up with boy band 5ive to play 'We Will Rock You' at the BRIT Awards. The subsequent single topped the charts that summer.

In 2001, May and Taylor collaborated with Robbie Williams to record 'We Are The Champions' for the movie, *A Knight's Tale*. Deacon uncharacteristically broke his silence to pronounce the version 'rubbish', but the Queen duo were enthusiastic enough to discuss the possibility of playing shows with Williams. However, somebody somewhere got cold feet and the plan was abandoned.

In June 2002, May had his own 'big moment' when he opened Her Majesty The Queen's Jubilee Concert, appearing on the roof of Buckingham Palace and playing his guitar version of the national anthem, supported by an orchestra, that he'd originally devised to close Queen's concerts nearly 30 years earlier. It was a symbolic indication of just how far rock music had come. Paul McCartney, Cliff Richard, Rod Stewart, Eric Clapton, Ray Davies, Phil Collins, Elton John, Tom Jones and Ozzy Osbourne were among the rock legends performing. Queen's contribution was 'Radio Ga Ga', with Taylor stepping out from behind his drum kit to handle the vocals.

## Breaking Free

In 2004, May and Taylor announced excitedly: 'Queen's phoenix is rising from the ashes'. They were teaming up with former Free and Bad Company vocalist Paul Rodgers. May and Rodgers had made occasional guest appearances with each other over the previous decade, but it was their collaboration at the Fender Stratocaster 50th Anniversary show in London earlier that year that really set the ball rolling.

Queen + Paul Rodgers, as they were billed, embarked on an 18-month world tour that was effectively a Queen/Free/Bad Company greatest hits show. Rodgers' instinctive blues voice was different from Mercury's more calculated tones, and he certainly didn't do camp, but he did bring a robust strength to Queen's songs. He also had to learn to harmonize. Their *Return Of The Champions* (2005) live album caught the full dynamics of their show, but their studio album, *The Cosmos Rocks* (2008), retreated to a safer, more formulaic style that was neither Queen nor Rodgers. The partnership was amicably dissolved in 2009.

## Looking For The X Factor

On the rebound from Paul Rodgers, May and Taylor were lured into *The X Factor* and *American Idol*, which could have compromised their integrity but instead led them to singer and Queen fan Adam Lambert, who was the runner-up on *American Idol* in 2009. He had auditioned with 'Bohemian Rhapsody' and ended up singing 'We Are The Champions' with May and Taylor in the show's finale. Lambert's subsequent US success as an openly gay singer impressed May and Taylor, who were all too aware that Mercury's overt gay behaviour was a significant factor in their failure to conquer America. After a well-received collaboration at the MTV Europe Music Awards in 2011, where they played a Queen medley, Queen + Adam Lambert made their concert debut in Kiev, Ukraine, in 2012, followed by shows in Russia, Poland and London. Lambert resumed his solo career, but rejoined Queen in September 2013 for a Las Vegas festival. In summer 2014, Queen + Adam Lambert embarked on an American tour, followed by dates in Asia and Australia.

# GAME OF THRONES

'[FREDDIE]
CELEBRATED
EVERY MINUTE.
AND, LIKE A
GREAT COMET,
HE LEFT A
LUMINOUS
TRAIL WHICH
WILL SPARKLE
FOR YEARS
TO COME.'
BRIAN MAY

Threatening to become even bigger than the band at one stage, Queen's musical We Will Rock You became one of the longest-running shows in London's West End, and eventually closed after 12 years in May 2014. More than 4,600 performances were seen by some 6.6 million people – one fan saw it 250 times – and the show has now travelled the world, boosting audiences up to 16 million.

## Stage Stars

The idea for a Queen musical began in 1996, and the original plan was to base it around the life of Freddie Mercury; however, this was rejected and comedian, novelist and writer Ben Elton was commissioned to write a script which was set in the future, in a world where rock and roll is banned.

When it opened in May 2002, it was the most expensive musical ever staged in London, at a cost of £6.5 million. It was savaged by the critics and early attendances were low, but May's appearance on the roof of Buckingham Palace a couple of months later produced a resurgence of interest in Queen and attendances soared. Throughout the 12-year life of the musical, both May and Taylor made regular unannounced appearances on stage.

## Freddie Forever

Another Queen album, using previously unheard Mercury vocals was released at the end of 2014. May says that more unreleased Mercury vocal tracks were uncovered, including some he recorded with Michael Jackson in the mid-1980s. May and Taylor worked on the tracks, adding guitar, drums and other instruments; May promised fans that the album will be both 'beautiful' and 'unusual'.

A Freddie Mercury biopic is set to start shooting in late 2014, despite delays caused by losing both the leading actor and director (Ben Wishaw is now playing the role of Freddie), as well as going through several script changes. The film, which was originally announced in 2010, will tell Mercury's story within the context of Queen, 'which was a kind of family', according to May. 'So it's about what happens in families, in a sense.'

## Queen Forever

Just what is it that makes the music of Queen so enduring? Many of the band's fans were not even born when Freddie

# 'NOTHING REALLY MATTERS,' ANYONE CAN SEE, NOTHING REALLY MATTERS, NOTHING REALLY MATTERS TO ME.'
## 'BOHEMIAN RHAPSODY'

Mercury died. Brian May thinks he might have some of the answers: 'We wrote as common people. We didn't write about what it means to be a rock star. We wrote about the dreams and fears and ambitions of everybody.'

He continues, 'There are songs like "I Want to Break Free", "We Are the Champions", "I Want It All" […] songs of people searching for a way out, a way to express themselves. […] You go to any football match or hockey match or English rugby match or whatever around the world and you will hear "We Will Rock You" and "We Are The Champions". They've become glued into people's everyday lives in a way that is much more powerful than what you have on a record in your collection. It kind of shocks me that we are still so current, but it's a very good feeling.'

*'There's a lot of freedom today and you can put yourself across any way you want to. But I haven't chosen this image. I'm myself and in fact half the time I let the wind take me.'*

*Freddie Mercury*

# FURTHER INFORMATION

## QUEEN VITAL INFO

### Freddie Mercury

| | |
|---|---|
| **Birth Name:** | Farrokh Bulsara |
| **Birth & Death Dates**: | 5 September 1946 |
| | –24 November 1991 |
| **Birth Place:** | Stone Town, Sultanate of Zanzibar |
| **Role:** | Lead vocalist, pianist |

### John Deacon

| | |
|---|---|
| **Birth Name:** | John Richard Deacon |
| **Birth Date:** | 19 August 1951 |
| **Birth Place:** | Oadby, Leicester, England |
| **Role:** | Bassist |

### Brian May

| | |
|---|---|
| **Birth Name:** | Brian Harold May |
| **Birth Date:** | 19 July 1947 |
| **Birth Place:** | Feltham, London, England |
| **Role:** | Guitarist, vocalist |

### Roger Taylor

| | |
|---|---|
| **Birth Name:** | Roger Meddows-Taylor |
| **Birth Date:** | 26 July 1949 |
| **Birth Place:** | King's Lynn, Norfolk, England |
| **Role:** | Drummer, vocalist |

# DISCOGRAPHY

## Albums (selected)

*Queen* (1973)

*Queen II* (1974)

*Sheer Heart Attack* (1974)

*A Night at the Opera* (1975)

*A Day at the Races* (1976)

*News of the World* (1977)

*Jazz* (1978)

*The Game* (1980)

*Flash Gordon* (1980)

*Hot Space* (1982)

*The Works* (1984)

*A Kind of Magic* (1986)

*The Miracle* (1989)

*Innuendo* (1991)

*Made in Heaven* (1995)

*Queen Forever* (2014)

## Singles (Selected)

| | |
|---|---|
| **1974:** | 'Killer Queen' (UK No. 2) |
| | 'Flick Of The Wrist' (UK No. 2) |

**1975:** 'Bohemian Rhapsody' (UK No. 1; US No. 9)

**1976:** 'You're My Best Friend' (UK No. 7)

'Somebody To Love' (UK No. 2)

**1977:** 'We Are The Champions' (UK No. 2; US No. 4)

'We Will Rock You' (UK No. 2; US No. 4)

**1979:** 'Don't Stop Me Now' (UK No. 9)

'Crazy Little Thing Called Love' (US No. 1; UK No. 2)

**1980:** 'Another One Bites The Dust' (US No. 1, UK No. 7)

'Flash' (UK No. 10)

**1981:** 'Under Pressure' (with David Bowie; UK No. 1)

**1984:** 'Radio Ga Ga' (UK No. 2)

'I Want To Break Free' (UK No. 3)

'It's A Hard Life' (UK No. 6)

**1985:** 'One Vision' (UK No. 7)

**1986:** 'A Kind Of Magic' (UK No. 3)

**1989:** 'I Want It All' (UK No. 3)

'Breakthru' (UK No. 7)

**1991:** 'Innuendo' (UK No. 1)

'Bohemian Rhapsody' (UK No. 1; US No. 2)

'These Are The Days Of Our Lives' (UK No. 1; US No. 2)

**1995:** 'Heaven For Everyone' (UK No. 2)

'A Winter's Tale' (UK No. 6)

**1996:** 'Let Me Live' (UK No. 9)

# AWARDS (SELECTED)

## American Music Awards
**1981:** Favorite Pop/Rock Single ('Another One Bites The Dust')

## BRIT Awards
**1977:** Best British Single of the Last 25 Years ('Bohemian Rhapsody')
**1990:** Outstanding Contribution to Music
**1992:** Posthumous Outstanding Contribution to Music (Freddie Mercury)
Best British Single ('These Are The Days Of Our Lives')

## Grammy Hall of Fame
**2004:** 'Bohemian Rhapsody' inducted into Grammy Hall of Fame
**2009:** 'We Will Rock You' and 'We Are the Champions' inducted into Grammy Hall of Fame

## Guinness World Records
**2002:** UK's Best Single of the Past 50 Years ('Bohemian Rhapsody')

## Hollywood Walk of Fame
**2002:** Band awarded a star on Hollywood Walk of Fame

## MTV Europe Music Awards
**2011:** Received the Global Icon Award

## Rock and Roll Hall of Fame
**2001:** Inducted into the Rock and Roll Hall of Fame

## Songwriters Hall of Fame
**2003:** The first band to be inducted into the Songwriters Hall of Fame

## UK Music Hall of Fame
**2004:** Inducted into the UK Music Hall of Fame

# ONLINE

**www.queenonline.com**: Visit Queen's official site for more information and a newsletter.

**www.queenworld.com:** Go to this site to find out how to join the Official International Queen Fan Club.

**www.facebook.com/queen:** With over 27 million likes, come here to for news and views on the band.

**twitter.com/queenrockband:** Head here for fast-paced updates about Queen.

**discuss.queenonline.com:** A forum for Queen fans to talk to other Queen fans across the world.

# BIOGRAPHIES

## Hugh Fielder

Hugh Fielder has been writing about rock and pop music for 35 years. He can remember the 1960s even though he was there. He can remember the 1970s and 1980s because he was at *Sounds* magazine (RIP) and the 1990s because he was editor of Tower Records' *TOP* magazine. He has shared a spliff with Bob Marley, a glass of wine with David Gilmour, a pint with Robert Plant, a cup of tea with Keith Richards and a frosty stare with Axl Rose. He has watched Mike Oldfield strip naked in front of him and Bobby Womack fall asleep while he was interviewing him.

## Mark Beaumont

Mark Beaumont (foreword) is an author, broadcaster and award-winning music writer for publications including *NME*, *The Guardian*, *The Times*, *Shortlist* and *Classic Rock*. He has

spent almost twenty years documenting the highs and lows of rock'n'roll's greatest names, interviewing everyone from Keith Richards and Paul McCartney to the biggest bands of today. He is the author of *Out Of This World: The Story Of Muse*, *Jay-Z: King Of America*, *Bon Iver: Good Winter* and *The Killers: Days & Ages* and his first novel *[6666666666]* is available on Kindle.

# PICTURE CREDITS

All images © **Getty Images** and the following: Terry O'Neill/Hulton Archive 1 & 40; Suzie Gibbons/Redferns 3 & 97 & 100 & back cover; Michael Putland/Hulton Archive 4, 9 & 13, 16, 106, 111; Gus Stewart/Redferns 7; Ian Dickson/Redferns 17 & 21, 39; Michael Ochs Archives 18, 61, 74; Mark and Colleen Hayward/Redferns 22, 25 & 30; David Redfern/Redferns 24, 66; Gijsbert Hanekroot/Redferns 32; Erica Echenberg/Redferns 33 & 36; Gary Merrin/Keystone/Hulton Archive 41 & 46; Fin Costello/Redferns 43; Richard E. Aaron/Redferns 49 & 52, 50; Keystone Features/Hulton Archive 55; Tom Hill/WireImage 57 & 62; Lex van Rossen/MAI/Redferns 59; Rob Verhorst/Redferns 65 & 68; The LIFE Picture Collection 72; Steve Jennings/WireImage 73 & 78; Larry Marano/Hulton Archive 80 , 81 & 85; Express Newspapers/Hulton Archive 82; Phil Dent/Redferns 86; Popperfoto 88, front cover & 94; Dave Hogan/Hulton Archive 89 & 90, 93, 96, 102, 104; John Rodgers/Redferns 105 & 108; Mick Hutson/Redferns 112, 117, 118; Junko Kimura/Getty Images Entertainment 113 & 114; Jeff Kravitz/FilmMagic 120; Ian Gavan/Getty Images Entertainment 121; Dave M. Benett/Getty Images Entertainment 122, 124; and © **REX** and the following: Ian Dickson 8; Keith Waldegrave/Associated 10; Linda Matlow 14; Ian Dickson 26; Andre Csillag 28; Everett Collection 35; Martyn Goddard 48; Eugene Adebari 56; Philip Dunn 64; Fraser Gray 70; Mark Mawson 77; Richard Young 98.